A
on L

Arthur Erickson on Learning Systems

With an introduction by Melanie O'Brian

Concordia University Press
Canadian Centre for Architecture
Montreal

Introduction by Melanie O'Brian

Arthur Erickson's Expanding Spaces   7
(and Systems) for Learning

Texts by Arthur Erickson

The University: 35
A New Visual Environment

Simon Fraser University   55

McGill University   69
Convocation Address

Arthur Erickson's Expanding Spaces (and Systems) for Learning

Melanie O'Brian

The texts by Arthur Erickson on learning systems collected here emphasize the critical role of the arts in pedagogy and how architecture operates as a structure for new ways of knowing.[1] Erickson, while grappling with the biases of Western education and its promotion of an individualized worldview, writes that architecture can guide institutions, such as in his design for Simon Fraser University (SFU), to integrate disciplinary studies and cultural perceptions toward innovation. Turning from a university system predicated on hierarchical and monastic retreat, Erickson instead considered the university as a reflexive and expanding learning system. He emphasized the intersection of bodies of knowledge and publics inside and outside the classroom to promote new disciplines emerging from between traditional ones.[2] He writes, "The purpose of architecture is not simply the provision of shelter or of giving that shelter an element of the aesthetic ... the purpose, as with any of the arts, is the demonstration to the culture of the meaning of its own environment."[3] Reflection is an important operation of the arts, by showing how culture—including the architectures of education—is articulated and therefore shaped.

As the former director and curator of SFU Galleries, spaces that enact the networked potential of the *curatorial*, I understand Erickson's writing process and formal architectural practice as attempts to integrate the world-making of an education system with experience. I see his expansive writing and his design's open geometry as akin to the conceptual and physical processes of contemporary art. The curatorial is used to describe research and material practices that link objects, images, methodologies, people, locations, histories, and discourses to reconfigure *how to know*.[4] It has come out of the field of art, but in its reorientation from inherited forms of knowledge to emergent forms (shaped by our current urgencies), the curatorial's methodology of becoming is applicable beyond art. Open-ended inquiry in education, which often emphasizes the critical competencies of the arts, sits uncomfortably against a current university ethos where skills and outcomes focus on training and professionalization.[5] The arts are underemphasized in the majority of today's learning environments, thus delimiting the possibilities of the interdisciplinary transformation proposed by Erickson.[6] Against today's universities—that are less sites of explorative inquisition and more marketplaces—Erickson's texts read as affirming and idealistic in their emphasis on the institution as a key determinant in shaping new knowledge. The grand terms and generalizations Erickson employs belie his own elite schooling; his thinking about education reform sits between patrician values and a widespread move to education for the masses.[7] Read together, his texts lead us through his process of looking back on SFU specifically. He asks: What is the university's role in culture? What is architecture's role? How is knowledge generated? What is a university's responsibility to a future? And he makes clear that if the university does not adequately question itself, it is the arts' role to do so.

Like other universities founded in the 1960s, SFU was a product of its time. It was enabled by cultural and countercultural shifts, as well as broader postwar socio-economic changes that saw more students attending university. In 1951 6.2 percent of the Canadian population had at one point been enrolled in undergraduate university programs. By 1964 this number grew to 12 percent, and by 2011 over 50 percent of the population held higher education credentials with 32 percent from university.[8] The province of British Columbia required a second public university in the metropolitan Vancouver region to meet demand and SFU, the so-called "instant university" or the "miracle on Burnaby mountain," opened in 1965 after two short years of design and building. Erickson and his design partner, Geoffrey Massey, submitted their concept for the architectural competition in 1963, and when it was chosen—based on an extraordinary proposal that included an educational rationale[9]— they worked with the four runners-up so each helped to design at least one building within the overall plan.[10]

Contextualized within a confluence of factors that included land, capital, political will, independence, and cultural experimentation that lead to SFU, Erickson's plan and writings on learning systems are propositional and maintain big-picture thinking. He emphasized functional spatiality over delineation by academic departments. This vision of the university as a single structure composed of numerous buildings and components foregrounds university architecture as a biological system that responds to and intersects with other systems, such as the larger metropolis and culture it is situated in, rather than a prescription for a resolved totality or finished form.[11]

In comparing a promotional guide prepared by SFU from 1966 with Erickson and Massey's SFU Development Plan from 1963, Erickson's contribution to *The Canadian Architect Yearbook* from 1965, Erickson's SFU Convocation Address from 1973, and his writing in the book *The Architecture of Arthur Erickson* from 1975,[12] Erickson's voice is distinctive and is used to speak for the university. He writes that he was, "carried away by revolutionary zeal—[and] proposed a return to the tutorial system modified for vast numbers of students."[13]

Erickson was working at a time when social and intellectual thought, including Marxism, systems theory, structuralism, and civil liberties activism revealed ideological determinations. His writing is disengaged from the particularities of these discourses but voiced the spirit of the time, as well as the biases that he promoted dismantling. SFU and other Canadian universities, such as Trent, were initiated when traditional academic ideas were already under scrutiny during a time when students protested for academic freedom and against the Vietnam War. While the ideologies of Herbert Marcuse and others were influential in the 1960s at SFU, in the following decade institutional politics reformed along disciplinary lines, and students faced uncertain job prospects—forces that contributed to a re-traditionalizing of the institution.[14] Erickson's writing is mythological, speaking in cultural generalities between East and West, and taking a long view that engages Socratic skepticism and the Platonic academy. Critical of the cloistered models of the universities of Oxford and Cambridge, Erickson's plan for SFU looked to the democratic eighth century Al-Azhar University embedded in the city of Cairo. He imagined a similarly public institution where students mixed not only with those in other fields, but also with those outside of academia. "There," Erickson writes, "students, scholars, merchants, beggars, gathered in groups seated on carpeted floors ... Anyone off the bustling streets of Cairo could stop in to listen to the soft discussion of medicine, law or the Koran, or to sleep in a corner if he wished."[15]

SFU's design was not a solution to a problem per se, but it clarified questions about how to address the gaps between traditional, elite learning and a public form that promoted new ways of thinking beyond siloed disciplines and social circles. Erickson saw the university as a system of belief that required constant questioning and referred warily to the "tutelage of the various shamans who preside over this secret society known as the university."[16] He understood the university, like the church or temple (SFU was an "appropriate Acropolis for our time"[17]), to have a spiritual mission toward knowledge production and to prepare students for the unknown.

The university as a mythic driver of civilization has been the subject of no small library of critique.[18] As much as postwar universities have fostered social movements for learning, research, and independent thought, they have also been caught up in capitalism's stream, emphasizing skills training over education that privileges critical debate, discussion, and nuanced thinking. Universities are increasingly specialized, making us, as Erickson writes (in problematic language), "brilliant in one field and abnormally retarded in all others. This 'idiot-savant' paradox could unfortunately characterize our civilization."[19] Erickson recognized the potential of the university but also saw the threats of professionalism, already at play in the 1960s, that accelerated in a neoliberal turn away from the humanities toward careerism and bureaucratic social engineering.[20]

The shape of SFU was determined by how its buildings express their hybridized and adaptable purpose for the future needs of an integrated whole. For this wicked problem, Erickson cut into the Burnaby mountain site, terracing rather than perching the buildings on the topography. By becoming part of the mountain, the composition of the university could be seen as a totality that formed along a spine (a mountain ridge) that allowed for organic expansion on the periphery without losing the whole. The plan was that, as SFU grew, new buildings of this living entity would remain tethered to the spine, keeping the campus's component parts architecturally connected—as well as to the natural world in the form of mountain-top views, meditative walks, intimate green spaces, and access to the surrounding forest. However, over the years the growing organism has worked less and less closely with the original design concept and it began to segregate departments, students, and faculty.[21] The ascent to the campus through the forest (and often the clouds, depending on the weather) remains exhilarating, but the impact of the site has changed: from the east entrance the monumentality of the campus is increasingly obscured by new buildings, the expansion is segmented rather than inte-grated, and trees impede the views. Additionally, campus pressures have resulted in the loss of original buildings that are not on the spine, such as the Erickson-designed Madge Hogarth House (originally the women's residence), to developer-driven designs of the late twentieth and twenty-first centuries for student residences, markethousing, and retail that are notable for their economy, functionality, and height, ringing the ridge-hugging centre.

Erickson and Massey's original SFU prospect-us framed learning as a result of the exchange of ideas and experience between professor and student, as well as with a wide variety of opinion, cultures, and publics that lie outside the class-room. It was noted that the idea of "inter-relationship was fundamental to [the] concept for Simon Fraser.

13

It was less important to show that Chemistry or Mathematics or Theatre or History were taught there than that knowledge in its infinite complexity was represented there for the advantage of the community." The university provided an "architectural environment conducive to such experiences, [that] demands a thoroughness and continuity of thought which can only occur as a result of close architectural control."[22] For Erickson, SFU would succeed in as far as it created relations between thinkers, activists, and citizens fixed in the wider life of a city: he conceived of SFU as an urban campus and emphasized an adjacent village.[23] Architectural control applied to the activity his built spaces determined, but also to the adjacencies and contexts they created.

The relevance Erickson placed on the role of the urban university, where it "can not be separated and isolated ... from the fabric of the city; nor can university training be separate from everyday existence,"[24] has not been achieved by the Burnaby campus. This is a foundational problem in terms of site: SFU will never be the urban campus that Erickson envisioned due to its remoteness from Vancouver and other regional centres, and a mountaintop university "village" is in process. Today SFU is designing more campus pockets that encourage lingering and intimate conversation, not only to accommodate an increased student population but also to address the transience of the campus commuters by encouraging "liveliness." While networked thinking is encouraged in this purpose-built environment, it is equally true that innovation is also born in poorly articulated, provisional spaces where chance meetings and discourses collide, meaning that architectural control is not an imperative to achieving such a goal. And the commons are increasingly virtual rather than physical. This drastically shifts our relationship to a centralized built environment. If it is debate, criticism, and exposure to unfamiliar perspectives that generates creativity, architectural design cannot always compete with happenstance physical proximity— nor virtual proximity—such as what occurred in Building 20 at the Massachusetts Institute of Technology in the 1940s, which is renowned for throwing seemingly unrelated groups together to result in legendary innovation: highspeed photography, the physics behind microwaves, Chomskyan linguistics, and the first video game.

Additionally, the SFU campus moves people rather than gathers them: the wide Mall, the expansive Academic Quadrangle, and the hallways work as canals rather than galvanizing interpersonal exchange. This may be due to scale and volume in part (the Mall, AQ, and hallways function best in ceremony and procession with their long modernist lines that direct movement), but also because the campus's remote, cool, damp climate, and the distances between transit, classrooms, and coffee shops increase a feeling of alienation.[25] With 2,500 students in 1965 and 30,000 attending today,[26] the architecture accommodates increased populations. The dense river of students that flow in sporadic currents of stillness and sprints along the wide hallways of the AQ creates a rhythm of sound, movement, and heat throughout the day. Despite their numbers, students appear to have a weaker claim to the university today compared to the 1960s when protests, sit-ins, occupations, and self-determination were central to SFU's ethos. Today, the collectivity of the student body operates across three campuses and may not need to lay claim to the physical site in the same way: a standalone Student Union Building is only now being built[27] and most students do not live on campus. Students are efficient with their time: habits of study, work, and communication have changed immensely due to technology and economic pressures. The Burnaby campus remains an architectural paradox. It was designed as a place for interaction while remaining an isolated site where most students do not participate in an active campus life.[28]

Campus spaces committed to interdisciplinary experience have become more limited as the university grew. For Erickson, the Library and Mall were examples of interdisciplinarity and central to the campus design. He voiced disappointment in their decentralization as the university expanded with increasing specialization.[29] Like the inquiry encouraged by the Library, the Burnaby campus's SFU Gallery in its modest, subterranean AQ home, remains a site that continues the ethos of the campus experience Erickson had envisioned: unaligned with an academic department,[30] contemporary, proprioceptive, social, intellectual, political, and process-driven. Erickson's skepti-optimism around the role of the university remains relevant, especially as the myth of the university as a community of free thinkers and world changers is replaced by a reality of professionalism. "It cannot be denied that the university is a place of refuge, and it cannot be accepted that the university is a place of enlightenment ... Is it not the purpose of the university as Universitas, as liberal arts, to make the commons, make the public, make the nation of democratic citizenry? Is it not therefore important to protect this Universitas, whatever its impurities, from professionalization in the university?"[31] The university may offer a retreat that withholds rather than expands—a debt/credit system that impedes expansive thinking.[32] Erickson's texts reveal developments in his thinking about learning systems—from idealistic in 1968 to disappointed in the 1980s—and how he was unprepared for the specialization of future disciplines and unwilling to problematize his own apolitically vague emphasis on interdisciplinarity and cultural exchange.[33]

How has SFU's, and Erickson's, original challenge to culture changed in our new era of dissent and transformation? When the globe is demanding massive reassessment in the face of climate emergency, systemic racial inequity, and so-called reconciliation with Indigenous peoples, the university offers an opportunity to re-evaluate both theory and practice predicated on the distinction between nature and culture to demand ecological and social justice. Erickson's vision for SFU hinged on the arts, intertextuality, cross-cultural connection, and sociality. In the 1960s art began leaving its sanctioned spaces, de-disciplining, making conceptual and formal breaks with modernism, and testing new conditions and audience relations. In SFU's early years, artistic creators and thinkers were an essential component of campus life resulting in the World Soundscape Project with R. Murray Schafer, visual art installations around campus including a curatorial project by Seth Siegelaub, and talks by R. Buckminster Fuller and Marcuse. Erickson, with his coterie, was also an instigator of cultural events.[34] When SFU's wild grassland fields were being mowed against his wishes, he enlisted the help of choreographer Helen Goodwin to spread poppy seeds over the grass. This mythological happening, a gathering that depended on the fluid line between art and life, was indicative of the cultural climate of the mid-1960s and of the community that felt responsible for SFU. The legacy of this time looms large for contemporary artists and thinkers who often mine the archive to reassess the '60s. At SFU Galleries, curatorial projects with artists Derya Akay and Julia Feyrer took up the story of the poppies, artists Sabine Bitter and Helmut Weber addressed the Templeton Five Affair,[35] and artists including Cedric Bomford, Andreas Bunte, Alex Morrison, and Samuel Roy-Bois considered the reverberations of Brutalism to query not only the social narratives put forward by the institution, but to question the larger complexities (and aesthetics) of its cultural identification.[36]

Erickson cautioned against the limits of knowledge acquired at the university and called for ways of learning outside the institution and outside the body of knowledge Western culture

perpetuates.[37] In the anthropocentric and cultur-
ally shifting moment of today, Erickson's writing
enables a review of what we have inherited
from modernity, including ideas of progress and
a categorical distinction between nature and
culture. Erickson's critique of fragmentation can
be seen to support an ecological worldview that
can take on speciesism, resituating non-humans
in the ethical and humans in the ecological.
In his acknowledgment of the rigged nature of the
dominance of Eurocentric knowledge over Black,
Indigenous, and people of colour's knowledges,
he recognized that the university's privileging
of certain forms of scholarship over others —
written over oral, history over memory, rationalism
over wisdom – has played a key role in ongoing
colonization. Erickson's call for interdisciplinarity
and contemporary calls for the institutional
inclusion and diversity of both bodies of knowledge and human bodies share a well-intentioned
but unproblematized interest in a future of greater
justice: "we hear the voices of the emerging
nations, and of our own native peoples, demanding to be heard ... They speak with increasing
doubt and misgiving about what we had always
held fervently to be the ultimate reality." And
he acknowledges that our reality is delivering "us
nearer universal calamity measured in terms of
pollution, resource depletion, and even extinction
of the very sources of life."[38] Erickson asserted
that if we can see the world as a construct, we can
ask questions of its economies, and we can find
ways to change the systems to reflect appropriate
needs. Despite failing to scrutinize the vagaries

of interdisciplinarity and the systems of power the university is predicated upon, Erickson's propositional thinking in the texts collected here, and his built work in its mission toward new knowledges, continue to provoke. Erickson writes that "The task the educator must face ... is not the inculcation of the known but the training for the unknown."[39]

The practices encompassed in the curatorial can be seen as analogous to Erickson's learning systems: both offer a porous network toward the emergence of new arrangements. Inherently speculative, both also require a physical enactment of theoretical premises in the form of a building, an exhibition in a gallery or a temporal happening at a specific site. The sheer scale and complexity of Erickson's architecture (for learning) has different stakes in terms of how it can continue to adapt and think itself forward. Erickson's SFU may have partially failed to follow his vision for a coherent living system, but in its adaption by other users it remains a biological system. Expansive thinking through curating makes "the curatorial the staging ground of the development of an insight in the making. These would be ideas or insights in the process of development, but subject to a different set of demands than they might bear in an academic context or in an activist context—not to conclude or to act, but rather to speculate and to draw out a new set of relations." When previous method-ologies are inadequate or inappropriate (such as revivalism for Erickson, or art history for curating), the curatorial determines its own structures and establishes itself as its own discipline without the limitations that academia and scholarly argument require. The possibilities of the curatorial are not only interdisciplinary but antidisciplinary—a critical and hospitable space for radical curatorial models and articulations of the politics of display both within the university and beyond. In creating a space of hospitality with the capacity to enlarge and open collective thinking against divisive or siloed imperatives, Erickson's writing and built work, like the curatorial, are shaping forces that shift our ethics and worldviews. They leave us with questions about who and what determines culture, how this is or is not changing, and what hold the university has on an uncertain horizon. Erickson's voice, in its enthusiasm and doubt, reminds us that architecture holds the ability to shape the activities it invites.

Notes

1   By *the arts* I mean to refer to the theory, application, and expression of creativity through technique and imagination in order to produce objects, environments, and experiences, such as architecture, visual art, literature, and performing arts. *Art*, as it is discussed in the field of contemporary art, may refer to (as borrowed from Irit Rogoff) collectables, displayables, cataloguables; artists and the politics of representation; operations of new modes of research to challenge knowledge production; the mimicking of structures or protocols to produce a critical gesture; a performative gesture of learning or urgency. In Rogoff's writing, art is "the ability to alert us to the emerging of a presence in the world." Irit Rogoff, "The Expanding Field," *Yishu* 13, 2, p. 14.

2   Erickson, "The University: A New Visual Environment," this volume, p. 44.

3   Ibid., p. 36.

4   Maria Lind first formalized the term *the curatorial* in "On the Curatorial," *Artforum*, Oct. 2009, 103.

5   James Elkins reflects on the under-emphasis of the arts in the university, especially around thinking through making, a methodology that does not easily align with other forms of university research. Elkins, "Afterword: Beyond Research and New Knowledge," in Katy Macleod, ed., *Thinking Through Art: Reflections on Art as Research* (London: Routledge, 2005), 245.

6   Interdisciplinarity is used by Erickson to describe disciplinary hybridity, cross-over, and multiplicity. A response to the limitations and narrow conventions of academic disciplines themselves through the critiques of modernism, for one, interdisciplinary thinking demanded an expanded taxonomical understanding, recognizing that specialist fields needn't be rigidly bounded so that the influence of other disciplines allows for new structures and networks of knowledge. By the 1950s, interdisciplinary thinking in the university was on the rise and, in some

debates, interdisciplinarity has collapsed with cultural theory. Erickson used this term uncritically. More specific terms, such as transdisciplinarity, which bridges a series of disciplines such that the work goes beyond any individual discipline or coupling of disciplines, are not interchangeable. For more on transdisciplinary research see Bill Seaman, "Combinatoric Micro-Strategies for Emergent Transdisciplinary Education," in Brad Buckley and John Conomos, eds., *Rethinking the Contemporary Art School: The Artist, the PhD, and the Academy* (Halifax: The Press of the Nova Scotia College of Art and Design, 2009).

7   Erickson was a student of the University of British Columbia and McGill University (graduating in 1950). He taught at UBC and at the University of Oregon, which privileged a Socratic, interdisciplinary methodology that saw students as part of the construction and exchange of knowledge rather than objects of instruction (Hugh Johnston, *Radical Campus: Making Simon Fraser University* [Vancouver: Douglas and McIntyre, 2005], 46).

8   See John Vanderkamp, "University Enrolment in Canada 1951–83 and Beyond," *The Canadian Journal of Higher Education* 4, 2 (1984), 51 and Daniel Munro, "Skills and Higher Education in Canada," *Canada2020.ca*, 2014, 8.

9   Johnston, *Radical Campus*, 48.

10   In 1963 Erickson joined forces with Massey and augmented Massey's staff at the New Design Gallery to prepare their plan (New Design Gallery is known as Vancouver's first commercial gallery, founded by Alvin Balkind who went on the direct UBC's Fine Art Gallery). The runners-up in the SFU architectural competition were William R. Rhone and Randle Iredale; Zoltan Kiss; Duncan McNab, Harry Lee, and David Logan; and Robert F. Harrison.

11   This volume, p. 39.

12   The promotional booklet produced by the university is "Simon Fraser University," edited by Edwin Turner (Vancouver: Evergreen Press, Oct. 1966), Canadian Centre for Architecture (CCA) Archives, Arthur Erickson fonds

ARCH279734; "Simon Fraser University Development Plan," prepared by Erickson / Massey Architects (Vancouver, BC: September 1963), CCA Archives, Arthur Erickson fonds, ARCH254999, reference number AP022.S1.1963.PR01; Arthur C. Erickson, "The Architectural Concept," *The Canadian Architect Yearbook 1965* (February 1966, vol. 11, no. 2), 40–41; Arthur Erickson, "Convocation Address for Simon Fraser University, 26 May 1973," CCA Archives, Arthur Erickson fonds, AP022.S1.1989.PR12; Arthur Erickson, *The Architecture of Arthur Erickson* (Toronto: Tundra Books, 1975).

13   This volume, p. 60.

14   Johnston, *Radical Campus*, 207.

15   This volume, p. 45.

16   This volume, p. 69.

17   Erickson, *Canadian Architect Yearbook 1965*, 41.

18   See, for example, Jerry Zaslove, "Imaginary Utopia, threatened idea," *SFU News*, 7 Sept. 2000 (vol. 19, no. 1); Mark Coté, Richard Day, and Greig de Peuter, eds., *Utopian Pedagogy: Radical Experiments Against Neoliberal Globalization* (Toronto: University of Toronto Press, 2007); and Maddie Breeze, Yvette Taylor, Christina Costa, eds., *Time and Space in the Neoliberal University* (Switzerland: Palgrave Macmillan, 2019).

19   This volume, p. 39.

20   Postwar emphasis in Western education on technological advances was a symptom of the Cold War. Governments invested more in universities and became interested in turning them away from traditional models toward utility and economic growth (Johnston, *Radical Campus*, 15). Thus universities become "enmeshed in the values of economy, mass production, and the rational bureaucratic state. If education is to be of any critical value in our world, it is vitally important to acknowledge that it should not be equated with intellectual and social conformity and the increasingly relentless regimes

of assessment and appraisal" (Brad Buckley and John Conomos, eds., *Rethinking the Contemporary Art School: The Artist, the PhD, and the Academy* [Halifax: The Press of the Nova Scotia College of Art and Design, 2009], 9).

21   This volume, p. 64.

22   "Simon Fraser University Development Plan," 17. CCA Archives, Arthur Erickson fonds, ARCH254999, reference number AP022.S1.1963.PR01.

23   Erickson's insistence on the relationship between the campus and the city for innovation may have informed the addition of two embedded urban campuses to SFU in Vancouver (1989) and Surrey (2002). "If the number of commuters could be reduced and a solid body of residents introduced, the university would gain a stability and liveliness that would enable it to offer a complete educational experience." This volume, p. 65.

24   This volume, p. 52.

25   Not to conflate the feelings of alienation determined by the architecture and those determined by the institutional system itself, it is notable that in summer sunshine SFU feels Arcadian, but on foggy winter days, its isolation and concrete feel penal.

26   30,000 students attend SFU across all three campuses.

27   The original Student Union Building was a provisional collection of small offices west of the library, integrated into the campus architecture. Erickson had originally envisioned a standalone student/faculty union building in a prime spot that was given over to a gas station. Students protested the gas station in the 1960s and Erickson wrote that "There was no building that could be targeted as 'theirs'" (this volume, p. 64).

28   SFU's Vancouver and Surrey campuses are integrated into their urban fabrics in a dozen or more buildings in the downtown core of the former, and in a Bing Thom high rise attached to a mall in the latter. These are examples

of urban integration that results in universities being active participants in city life and vice versa.

29   This volume, pp. 38–39.

30   SFU has no art history department and the School for the Contemporary Arts moved off the Burnaby campus to Vancouver in 2010.

31   Stefano Harney and Fred Moten, *The Undercommons: Fugitive Planning and Black Study* (Wivenhoe, UK: Minor Compositions, 2013): 26, 30.

32   Harney and Moten refer to refuge as a place of debt and define debt as mutual: "The place of refuge is the place to which you can only owe more, because there is no creditor, no payment possible" ("Debt and Study," *eflux journal* 14, Mar. 2010).

33   This doubt crept into his thinking in the 1970s: "Even the design of this university for better or worse was an attempt to put the heretofore fragmented university campus back together again, in the hopes that the gaps between the separate intellectual disciplines themselves might be bridged." Erickson, "Convocation Address for Simon Fraser University," May 26, 1973, 6, CCA Archives, Arthur Erickson fonds, AP022.S1.1989.PR12.

34   Erickson was closely connected to Vancouver's art community, particularly to Lawren Harris, B.C. Binning, and Gordon Smith (who undertook large-scale mosaic murals for the new SFU campus).

35   In 1967 five SFU teaching assistants led a demonstration at Templeton Secondary School demanding academic freedom in response to high school students that were suspended for distributing a publication that mocked a teacher's view of poetry. The TAs were penalized for organizing the protest and this escalated into a student demonstration at Convocation Mall's Freedom Square.

36   Derya Akay and Julia Feyrer's project was part of the SFU Galleries' group exhibition *Geometry of Knowing* (2015) and was held at SFU Gallery and offsite. Sabine

Bitter and Helmut Weber's *The Templeton Five Affair, March 1967* (2010) was part of the SFU Galleries' group exhibition *Through a Window: Visual Art and SFU 1965–2015* (2015) and was held at the Teck Gallery. Cedric Bomford's *Mountain Embassy* (2019) was held at SFU Gallery and offsite. Andreas Bunte's *Erosion* (2016) was held at SFU Gallery. Alex Morrison's *Phantoms of a Utopian Will / Like Most Follies, More Than a Joke and More Than a Whim* (2015) was held at SFU Gallery and Burnaby Art Gallery. Samuel Roy-Bois's *Not a new world, just an old trick* (2013) was held at SFU Gallery. For details, see sfugalleries.ca (accessed 4 Feb. 2021).

37   SFU's motto for engagement is a current manifestation of Erickson's vision, in which the institution emphasizes the role the university has to play in communities and how community-engaged research inflects back on the institution. SFU's current Strategic Vision focuses on "Engaging Students, Research and Communities," https://www.sfu.ca/content/dam/sfu/engage/StrategicVision.pdf (accessed 6 Feb. 2021).

38   This volume, p. 73.

39   This volume, p. 44.

40   Rogoff, "The Expanding Field," 17.

Erickson / Massey Architects, topographical plan detailing the interconnected spaces of Simon Fraser University, Burnaby, British Columbia. Competition drawing, ca. 1964.

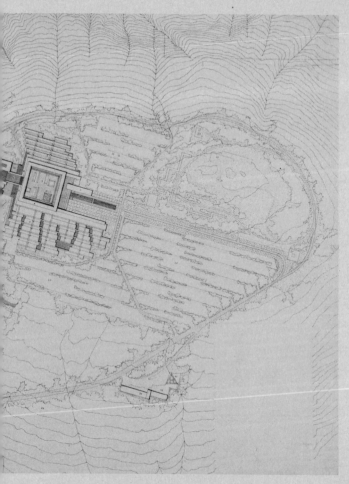

Set atop Burnaby Mountain, the campus is organized around the
Academic Quadrangle and along the east-west Mall axis.

Graphite and ink on translucent paper, 65.7 × 107 cm.
Arthur Erickson fonds, CCA Collection, ARCH252721.
Gift of the Erickson Family.

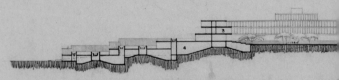

SECTION 2 · THRU CLASSROOMS, FACULTY OFFICES, ACADEMI
SCALE: 1" = 50'

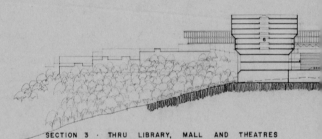

SECTION 3 · THRU LIBRARY, MALL AND THEATRES
SCALE: 1" = 50'

SECTION 4 · THRU STUDENT UNION, MALL AND GYMNASIUM
SCALE: 1" = 50'

Erickson / Massey Architects, fragment of a competition
drawing presenting perspectives and sections of the
Simon Fraser University project, ca. 1964.

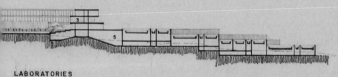

LABORATORIES

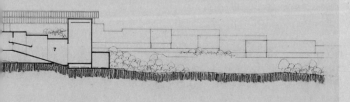

Top: Section through classrooms, faculty offices,
Academic Quadrangle, and laboratories.

Middle: Section through Simon Fraser University
library, Mall, and theatres.

Bottom: Section through Student Union,
Mall, and gymnasium.

Site for the construction of the Simon Fraser University Burnaby campus,
20 November 1963. Photograph by George Allen

Bird's-eye view, Simon Fraser University Burnaby campus, 20 July 1966.
Photograph by George Allen

Simon Fraser University, Presentation booklet (October 1966), page 4.
Arthur Erickson fonds, CCA Collection, ARCH279734.

A Note on the Texts

Small stylistic changes for punctuation and to correct typographical mistakes have been made to the text without being marked. Additions for clarity or for missing words in Arthur Erickson's texts are included in square brackets. Notes in Arthur Erickson's writings to include citations and contextual information have been added by the publisher.

"The University: A New Visual Environment," is an edited version of Erickson's Frank Gerstein Lecture at York University, Toronto, 9 November 1967, that was published in *Canadian Architect* 13, 1 (January 1968), pp. 26–37.

"Simon Fraser University," is a previously unpublished text that appears to have been written for a public talk but the provenance is uncertain, as is the date. However, based on references Erickson makes to additional building on the SFU campus, it seems likely it was written sometime after 1981. CCA Collection, Arthur Erickson Fonds, ARCH257571, collection number: AP022.S2.SS1.D6.

The last piece is a previously unpublished text for a convocation ceremony address delivered by Arthur Erickson at McGill University on 5 November 1975. CCA Collection, Arthur Erickson Fonds: BIB 211877.

The University:
A New Visual Environment

Architecture is no more than a reflection of the
concepts of the culture behind it. It is language,
a visual one, which envelops and acts upon
us at all times. It is fundamental to the growth
and continuity of a culture and at the same
time it is the most complete and telling evidence
of its nature. Architecture is a language as
complex as the verbal language, ranging from
crude exclamations to philosophical elabora-
tions and poetic insights. It can speak to us
rudely, logically or eloquently. In scope it can
involve so much of the man-made environment
that "architecture" is no longer a word comprehensive enough to encompass the concerns of
the designer today. Like any language, architecture is heir to the existing cultural pattern. Its
limitation—and at the same time its basis—is
the intellectual and spiritual milieu of the time.
We are destined always to reinterpret history in
the terms of our immediate values, since form,
after all, is in the eye of the beholder.

Thus architecture is not the creature of
unbridled imagination but a statement of what
exists. The architect is not so much a form-
maker as a diviner of forms that would emerge.
His abilities are merely a keener sensitivity to
an environmental need and the drive to fulfil

that need. He is always faced with myriad conditions impinging on his subject, and the more comprehensive his grasp of these, the more penetrating and universal his consensus. The purpose of architecture is not simply the provision of shelter or of giving that shelter an element of the aesthetic, although both can be consequences. The purpose, as with any of the arts, is the demonstration to the culture of the meaning of its own environment. It is by this that we sense the reasons for what we do and begin to know what we are.

Medieval man could not, in any sense, accept the thought or environment of our times, just as we cannot really penetrate the mind of medieval man. It is difficult for us to conceive of a culture where, for example, the individual in our sense was non-existent, where religion was science, where painting, sculpture and architecture were not even recognized as separate arts, and where no building could be singled out from the total matrix of the town. The medieval city was a tightly interknit "megastructure" with each piece fitting so well that there was no indication of separation or of independent purpose. Even the proud cathedral was only an outgrowth and culmination of the town.

In the 14th century man became interested in the physical world around him and initiated "individualism." For the first time, he began to separate himself from his surroundings. *Perspective* came from *per specare*— to see clearly. The concern of the designer was to separate and to describe distinctly objects

in their unique and individual positions
in space. At the same time early science, in its
observation of the same surroundings, began
to view and to divide natural phenomena into
different parts for the isolation and examination of behaviour. Soon the tree, which in
the 11th century had been a divine manifestation, image of the seasons, bearer of fruit,
was to become a functioning system of root
hairs, cambium and chlorophyll—an ingenious
production plant from a mechanistic point
of view. Nature was no longer a divinely moti-
vated whole in the medieval sense, but a sum
of functioning parts.

This urge to particularize extended into
every aspect of life and supported the 19th and
20th century concept of individualism. We have
come so far in our particularization of phenomena that we see the individual as self-determined
and functioning separately from a society whose
purpose as a whole is no longer evident. In
architecture this particularization accounts for
separate, independent buildings which, thrown
together, make up the modern city of no particular consequence.

This approach—seeing nature as a collection
of functioning parts—was the preparation
for human prowess in the invention of machines.
Observing how things worked, we could dupli-
cate the method. If we had not developed this
mechanistic view of nature, we would not have
been able to devise nature's mechanical count-
erparts. The human body soon became extended
into mechanical eyes, ears, mouth and legs—or

optical devices, television, telephone, radio, automobiles. Progress in technology has matched progress in biological analysis; only with knowledge of the brain were we able to invent the computer and to provide a mechanical counterpart to that part of the body.

In North America these cultural haracteristics developed a particular form due in part to an initial commitment to the conquest and organization of the land. The early pioneer had to settle the land—clear it, tame it, recultivate it. The land was hostile, and progress could be achieved only with destruction and replacement. Newness became a manifestation of fresh conquest; became a fundamental symbol of our culture. Newness is a constituent part of our aesthetic sense—new styles, new ideas, new ears, fresh paint, clean and shiny surfaces, chrome, plastic, and youth at all costs.

As pioneers we were forced to develop ingenuity and self-reliance. Inventions and labour-saving devices came out of the American farmstead. American ingenuity and organizational ability became cultural characteristics. In early society where end results were often of critical importance to survival, quantitative rather than qualitative values became dominant. Possession became associated with success and developed the trend towards the materialistic side of human endeavour. As science and mechanical prowess evolved hand in hand, specialization became a necessary condition of competence and erudition. Both the necessity and the glamour of specialization had a profound effect on our view of all aspects of life. The result is that we have developed a culture that has that characteristics of a person who is brilliant in one field and abnormally retarded in all others. This "idiot-savant" paradox could unfortunately characterize our civilization. Although we are about to land on the moon, an incredible feat of science and technology, in the regions of human sensibility and the human institutions devised to act on behalf of this sensibility—in religion, art, law, education and government—we are eons behind our technology.

"Functionalism" is so completely built into our responses that we are unable to divorce ourselves from its domination of our thinking. We think of natural organisms as functioning systems whereas it would be better to think ofartificial systems, such as buildings and even cities, as organisms. The conception of a building, or of a building complex, as a biological system requires that its form not only be the result of its own inner necessities but that it reflect the modification and adaptation of all biological systems to the outer influences of their environment. Thus the building complex, though one of a species, becomes a variation of the species through the influence of its surroundings. If all those shaping the environment—the developer, the engineer, the planner, the architect—responded equally to such an ecological approach, our cities and our universities might be less chaotic and yet more diversified, with a biological appropriateness throughout.

Systems thinking has several limitations. Man is not the colour of his eyes, hair, skin or the shape of his nose: these may define a particular appearance. Man is a particular arrangement of parts—a particular system in which there is little variation. But that is not enough to answer the question "what is man?" The pursuit of the answer to that question is one of our major preoccupations. Similarly the pursuit of that answer in the realm of man's artifacts is the greatest preoccupation of the designer. In asking "what is it?" a designer approaches but never finds the answer. A design can never be a solution to a problem; it can only attempt to clarify the question. The time when the question is no longer asked signals a kind of atrophy or "hang-up" in design. This state becomes evident in a disproportionate emphasis on appearance or styling.

In recent years, for instance, there has been very little basic change in the automobile—new models have concentrated rather on fashion, on the styling of an old stereotype. Aircraft, on the other hand, show less concern with style because they are still involved in the quest. The early one-passenger aircraft with elaborate wing superstructure is quite another vehicle from a hundred-passenger jet with the body and wing hardly differentiated from each other. In both cases we are speaking of vehicles—and vehicles are designed for a performance that can more or less explicitly be described. Vehicles must get one there, and all other factors are subject to this.

The static structures of land are not as simply defined in these terms of performance as Buckminster Fuller would have them be. As elegant as is the structure of the American pavilion at Expo, it is unimpressive in all other aspects of accommodation except shelter.[1] In the category of human structures one must compare it to the igloo or the tepee—each as brilliant and elegant a solution to their needs according to their techniques as is Fuller's dome with respect to his incomparably superior technology.

Structure, though essential, is only one of the many aspects of the problem of human accommodation. When primitive societies evolved so that other motivations than survival entered their existence, their habitation became as differentiated and complex as their culture would allow. The dwelling was not merely an ingenious device for shelter, but a symbol of the domicile: nor was a storehouse merely a device for storing grain, nor a meeting hall for gathering for council, nor a temple for offering thanksgiving—but, as well, each expressed its purpose. Thus an elaborate language of form was established and has increased in complexity as social organization and motivations have evolved.

The language was clear until technology began to dominate human institutions, and as with any primitive society with a new tool, it is taking us time to use the tool expressively. In the modern city it is difficult to discern any language at all, because it is hardly developed in terms of our technology. It is there, however, though as yet unrecognized or ill-said. Recent movements in art—op, pop and kinetic—show a discovery of some of the new words that have come into the visual vocabulary. They are a refreshing sign that we are becoming aware of the culture that the 20th century has created, no matter how we appraise it, and are enjoying it perhaps for the first time.

Out of the complex variety of this century's buildings, a few archetypes have emerged. Like the automobile, the office building has long been solved and is only open to stylistic variations until the premise is changed. It is an inhuman but supremely rational resolution of real estate subdivision, the economics of costs and rental returns, the potentials of vertical transportation and the pattern of the modern office organization. It is also, in its sterility and intense practicality, a fair commentary on the civilization that produced it.

The dwelling, however, has not found its 20th century definition. Until now the mass dwelling or apartment has been nothing more than an office building stacked around an elevator tower, differentiated only by the addition of individual kitchens and plumbing.

And what about the university? Major change is apparent in many fields and seems to herald a new understanding about the potential as well as about the limitations of our own immediate culture. Every moment we are becoming more aware of what seems to constitute the particular tenor of our civilization and thus are moving away from it. Protest movements and flower children are a small evidence of change. Sacred cows are being slaughtered one by one; life is quickly coming to demand complete immersion, without qualification of prejudgment, into the immediate scene.

Such changes challenge the institutions designed to perpetuate the culture—that is the very basis of the educational system. In a culture with prescribed goals, one could "measure up" and be assessed, but how can one set such plateaux in a constantly changing situation? Since the development of the computer we have finally been convinced about the fallibility of treating the human mind as a memory bank to be fed with facts and tested. Without the computer we might have continued to believe that our particular human distinction was the superior logic of our brain and continued to assess our civilization on these grounds. But the computer has suddenly wrenched that distinction from us and we are forced to turn to other aspects of our humanity to have our self-respect.

The effect of the computer on education is important not only in the area of information retrieval and problem-solving, but in changing the whole direction of education. As Marshall McLuhan observes, because a worldwide network of computers will make all of man's factual knowledge available to students everywhere, "the human brain will not have to serve as a repository of specific facts and the uses of memory will shift."[2] Memory in fact might

become a hindrance rather than a help. There
are other higher orders of intelligence that
break through the bonds of memory to new
patterns of thought.

The task the educator must face, then, is
not the inculcation of the known but the training
for the unknown. The student must have the
intelligence to take advantage of the unpredictable. The body of knowledge will hardly
be relevant when the "memory bank" will be a
readily available source of information for
everyone. Then, the emphasis in education
might shift from the imparting of knowledge to
its real function—enlightened experience. Then,
the examination might be like the riddle set by
the Zen master; when the novice tries to answer
with his logic he strikes him with a paddle
and only rewards him when he answers with
perception—and the reward is yet another riddle.
"What is the sound of one hand clapping?"

Today, any intelligent youth knows he
doesn't need a teacher in the traditional sense,
and that he hardly needs a university in the
traditional sense. He does need, however,
resources—vast resources, readily available,
in a convenient way, the freedom to follow
his own conscience and curiosity, and contact
with others, both more experienced and less experienced than himself, who are engaged as he is,
in the adventure of learning. All a university
need be is any place where this can happen. With
Socrates it occurred under a tree, with Plato,
on either side of a wall. With the first medieval
scholastics it was the retreat from world into

monastic "closes." But the American university, so suitable to specialization and mass-production has its prototype campus been, has hardly been questioned at all. However, its obvious shortcomings in meeting the present situation force us to ask again "What is the university?"

A university as an organism, in a bio-architectural way of speaking, differs in organization, purpose and method from place to place, and its physical form is a direct outcome of its educational point of view and its needs. To use only an aesthetic excuse for the placing of buildings, such as the fact that they look well in a park-like setting, is to misunderstand the role of architecture and to misinterpret the purpose of the university. There was no random choice in Plato's wall or Oxford's New College, but a very specific organization of space tailored to a very precise concept of education.

Perhaps the first "university" was that of Al-Azhar in Cairo in the 9th century—the great centre of Islamic teaching. There students, scholars, merchants, beggars, gathered in groups seated on carpeted floors, shuttered from the blazing light of the courtyard. Anyone off the bustling streets of Cairo could stop in to listen to the soft discussion of medicine, law or the Koran, or to sleep in a corner if he wished. But it was the centre of the Islamic culture which dominated the Mediterranean until the 13th century.

The early colleges of Oxford or Cambridge are equally strong statements of the kind of retreat requisite to education in their time. Patterned after the medieval monastery, which was archetypal in its design for study and reflection, buildings were arranged around the mingling space of the quadrangle and the monastic cloister. In contrast to the urban setting of the University of Paris, the English colleges were residential and introverted. In the discipline of the college day there was a fusion of instruction with worship, sport and social contact. The buildings, whether residences, dining hall or chapel, were continuous structures around the quadrangle and cloister, with the chapel dominating the complex as it dominated the goals of the early university.

The English pattern persisted in the early colleges of America. However, as the university gradually became a public institution focused on mass education, the pattern changed, with the residence a minor provision and classroom the most important element of the campus. With the fragmenting of studies and the departmental organization devised to administer these, the blocks of classrooms developed, in effect, into isolated colleges devoted to one particular branch of knowledge. These in turn began to be specialized in form to accommodate the particular needs of the subject in question and to be scattered in their own plot of land to allow for expansion. Dormitories, an isolated function, were set in separate buildings apart from the teaching campus, the vestige of the chapel was perhaps a bell tower and the replacement in importance was the administration building.

The North American campus became in prototype a field in which were placed at random separate buildings for separate studies—each having little regard for the others and the whole being organized after no evident pattern or purpose. It was democratic, individualistic, fragmented in the extreme. It had little to do with the ideals of education but was concerned with the highly organized process of departmental indoctrination. New universities are being planned in this manner even at this moment.

Today, few disagree that there is a great deal of confusion in university planning. Planners, divorced from the understanding of educational aims, resort to arbitrary planning devices to tie the mass of buildings together. But all of these are superficial to essential planning problems and are applicable only when the university itself is floundering with respect to its goals.

The new visual environment of the university can be no more than what the university professes. Certainly there has not recently been an environment that has reflected as strong a viewpoint as Al-Azhar, Oxford or Cambridge. And we must learn to accept the importance of the environment as a major contribution to the educational experience. One needn't go as far as those who claim that with the right environment the rest will take care of itself, but its potential can no longer be underestimated.

The major common problem that faces all universities today, whatever their policy, is that of growth. In this respect the university is the most complex of all modern institutions because each faculty and department has a different rate and pattern of growth and must be accommodated. The problem is made especially difficult because it is impossible to anticipate accurately how great the expansion will be, where it will occur, and also in what academic direction the university will flourish. Therefore the university plan must allow for growth in any and all directions—in effect, must be as open-ended and non-structured as possible. The traditional American campus solved this problem by scattering faculties over the campus and allowing for growth between. But such an unreasonably extended campus is continually disrupted by its building program, in styles and accommodation that defeat its original intention.

In the United States, the question of the new environment has not been asked too insistently—perhaps because of the entrenched system. Some consolidation of scattered buildings was attempted at the Air Force Academy in Colorado.[3] More recently, Chicago Circle University attempted to classify space rather than disciplines in order to provide for the critical problems of growth, change, the efficient use of space and the economy of construction.[4] There, all offices are in one type of building, classrooms in another and labs in another, allowing for common use, the borrowing and lending of facilities among departments, and an inter-relationship of disciplines.

In Canada, Simon Fraser [University] went further by bringing the concept of compact multi-use space into a single megastructure—a university arranged horizontally along a central spine which accommodates all services, covered pedestrian traffic and parking. In Simon Fraser the problem of expansion was answered by establishing a spine which was fixed and unchanging from which growth would occur on the periphery when and where necessary, without disturbing the central core of the university. Since most growth occurs in the lab and lecture areas, these were relegated to either side of a quadrangle at the top of the campus. At the same time, there was an effort to make all space anonymous and interconnected so as to provide for the greatest possible interchange among the various disciplines. The spine, which is the heart and circulation system of the university, provides areas for student communication and contemplation—the busy mall, the quiet quadrangle.

Whereas Simon Fraser is a chain of events along the spine, Scarborough went further in eliminating altogether the identities of different parts.[5] Not having quite the problems of a major university, Scarborough was able to meld all the differing accommodation of the college— classrooms, laboratories, library, offices, cafeteria, lounges, etc.—into one continuous complex. Since all labs and classrooms are completely convertible, they can be programmed for any department. Expansion is achieved quite simply at either end. Whereas Simon Fraser is linked by a spine which presents a series of exterior courts to the pedestrian, Scarborough is built

around a continuous interior street that expands
and contracts, allowing for lounges and meeting
places along its length, each in its way an adaptation to different climates.

Trent [University] another distinctive
Canadian example, poses the point of view that
education develops in the cultivating atmosphere
of a small residential group. This reflects the
philosophy of the English college system, with
the difference that Trent is a serious attempt to
meet North American demands as well.

In England, the tradition of the residential college for the elite is so strong that it still
dominates in one form or another the plans
of new universities. This is emphasized by the
fact that many of the architects themselves are
graduates of the old colleges. With a smaller
enrollment than the vast American universities
and without serious parking demands, the
pressure to devise new solutions has not been
so great. One of the most interesting designs
nowin construction is that of the University
of East Anglia by Denys Lasdun.[6] In his plan
growth occurs out along many fingers, each
finger representing a major division of study:
chemistry, biology, physics, arts, social sciences,
etc. Residences are tied into the complex as
in the traditional English university (seventy-five
percent of the students will be in residence)
and the whole complex is interconnected and
radiates out from the central core containing
the library and university house. This pattern
is radically different from that of the traditional
courtyard complex. East Anglia embodies what

is required of it: that individual disciplines not be housed in separate departments but grouped into "broadly based schools of study conceived as the basic socio-academic activities of the University."[7] Living in lodgings is to be less important than university life with a library, labs and common rooms open for long periods seven days a week.

In Germany, the competition for Bochum University elicited a number of farsighted schemes based on the pedestrian spine as discussed above, or on huge parking decks out of which the buildings rise.[8] None of these plans, though competent, advances quite the important step in planning that is evident in the German Free University scheme, by Candilis, Josic and Woods.[9] This university departs from the single spine system which is evident in all the latter universities we have discussed except Trent. Instead, it is based on several parallel spines, which are the traffic and service systems of the university. On each of these spines are nodes, which are departmental centres or major lecture or theatre centres. These are allowed to expand in several directions filling in the space between the spines, creating a cross-street system. The growth is similar to that of a town where a traffic system is laid out and growth occurs in a haphazard manner as the need occurs. The result is a kind of highly built-up town. Obviously, it is a plan devised for an urban centre. It would fit well in the downtown of any city, for it is a kind of downtown in itself. And here is the seed of the next possible stage of development—the university completely absorbed within the city pattern—in a sense the non-university.

Today the university is perhaps the most complex of all modern institutions. Its role is being challenged and its destiny is in the balance. It is a micro-city of many subcultures, of highly specialized needs and unpredictable growth. It is a city of thirty thousand persons but could be one of two hundred thousand persons or more. Many of the problems that face the modern metropolis are common to the university as well. Experiments in university planning can even bear fruit in new towns because more and more the needs of the university and the solutions to these needs are the solutions common to any urban situation.

At the same time that the university is becoming more a part of the public domain, it is also engaged more critically in the life of the community. We may find in the not too distant future that the last boundaries of fragmentation are broken down—that the university can not be separated and isolated, as has most often been the case, from the fabric of the city; nor can university training be separate from everyday existence. The development of electronic teaching devices and memory banks may make it possible for the future university to be truly a university in the sense that it involves everyone and his entire life. University training may not engage a particular period in our lives but involve us continuously, so that our experience of life and our knowledge of it develop

hand in hand. Thus our lives might be lived
out in a university which is, in effect, the very
heart of the city. There would be no mayor
nor council for a city, but perhaps a university
president and senate.

Whatever the destiny of the university
it is important that the urban role be realized.
In spite of electronic means of communication,
it is ultimately the actual mingling of people
in a common centre that is essential to the
development of a civilization. The university
might be the last place that can provide this centre—and potentially the greatest resource ever
provided by mankind. I can only see its effect
on our lives and our involvement with it increasing, though it will be very different in the future
from what it is now. It could be to us what the
church was to medieval man—the very core
of his existence and the culmination of the city.

The university to come may again be
as direct a solution as Plato's wall to the need
for knowledge, at any time, in any manner one
wishes. But architecture is a slave to attitudes—
it provides for and reflects the immediate
occasion. Great architecture only penetrates
more deeply into that moment.

Notes

1   Erickson refers to the geodesic dome designed by architect R. Buckminster Fuller (1895–1983) for the US pavilion at Expo 67 in Montreal.

2   Marshall McLuhan and George B. Leonard, "The Future of Education: The Class of 1989," *Look Magazine* (21 February 1967), 25.

3   Designed by Walter Netsch (1920–2008) for Skidmore, Owings, and Merrill (SOM), construction started in 1954 and was completed in 1964.

4   Erickson refers to the University of Illinois at Chicago Circle campus, of which Walter Netsch was the lead architect for SOM. Construction began in 1963 and the campus opened in 1965.

5   Erickson refers to the campus of University of Toronto, Scarborough, designed by John Andrews (1933–) and constructed from 1963 to 1964.

6   Denys Lasdun (1914–2001), English architect.

7   While we are unable to identify the source of this quotation, based on the context of Erickson's discussion, it seems likely to be related to either the specifications of the University of East Anglia's architectural competition or perhaps a statement of intentions by Lasdun.

8   The competition for the campus of Ruhr-University Bochum was held in 1962 and it was awarded to Helmut Hentrich (1905–2001). The university was founded in 1962 and instruction began in 1965.

9   Georges Candilis (1913–1995), Alexis Josic (1921–2011), Shadrach Woods (1923–1973), and Manfred Schiedhelm (1934–2011) won the design competition for the Free University of Berlin in 1963.

Simon Fraser University

Recalling distant events is not easy, but those years two decades ago were momentous ones that changed my life, and certain experiences will always be vividly remembered.

When the competition for Simon Fraser University was announced, I was an assistant professor at the School of Architecture at the University of British Columbia, keeping architectural skills alive doing a few small houses.[1] Conveniently, the competition would fill the summer break and finish by the beginning of the fall semester. I had no base to do the competition myself so I joined forces with Geoff Massey, a loyal friend with whom I had done a couple of houses. We augmented his staff at the New Design Gallery on Pender Street with the brightest of the graduating students and headed into the most frantic summer any of us had known.

The competition instructions had been very specific about the location of five buildings— an arts building, a science facility, library, theatre and gymnasium—as separate units on top of Burnaby Mountain. This requirement reflected the contemporary North American concept of the university as an umbrella for many specialized areas of knowledge, with faculties isolated in separate physical plants. To me, that concept existed for bureaucratic convenience rather than educational goals, and at the same time echoed Newton's mechanistic view of knowledge rather than Einstein's theory that all was connected.

I was more than an armchair skeptic about the evils of North American campuses. I had been teaching for several years. My thesis at McGill School of Architecture had dealt with New College, Oxford, and the earliest universities. [I planned after my] graduation to visit them all: Al-Azhar, Salamanca, Paris, Oxford, and Cambridge. They all seemed to embody a philosophy of education in which all knowledge was related and all its seekers—professors and youths alike—members of one community. Al-Azhar, with its tranquil courtyards and vast carpeted mosque where classes gathered almost informally about the muezzin, epitomized the intimacy of teacher and student. The Oxbridge colleges, with their purposeful, carved-out court spaces between dormitory and dining hall, and cloister connecting great hall and chapel, embodied a whole cycle involving equally intellectual, spiritual and physical pursuits.

We began by looking at the common spatial denominators of all SFU's faculties: auditoria, classrooms, seminar rooms, offices and laboratories. We saw that these need not be set up separately, but could be grouped in common, respecting administrative territories but taking advantage of economies in construction by mating like structures and services. This would automatically provide linkage of faculties and would encourage the growth and accommodation of the new disciplines then proliferating in the gaps between the traditional ones.

Approaching the problem of what form these new groups would take, I saw the opportunity to recreate the educational spaces so characteristic of the older universities. My own experience had taught me that knowledge was transferred as much outside the confines of the classroom as within. The right spaces would encourage those encounters. The mealtime discussion, the thoughtful stroll in the garden, the argument in the lounge— all this was seldom provided for in the utilitarian, force-feeding approach of the new universities of North America. We came up with four categories of educational spaces.

First of all, it was obvious that there needed to be a primary space at the crossroads of the university, the place of widest interaction between students adjacent to the library and eating facilities. Respecting Burnaby's climate, this generated the idea for the covered Mall. The second space needed to be a counterpart to the Oxbridge quadrangle and would balance the busy Mall. The space would be tranquil, an area one could stroll in, talk and think—perambulation being recognized by both Buddhism and Christianity as conducive to deep thought. The mere preoccupation with repetitive movement in quiet circumstances frees the mind to probe and roam. Here was evoked the classic pattern of the monastery with its covered arcade of rhythmic repetition, its changing view of a garden and the sound of water. In our Academic Quadrangle there would be no variation in the

monotonous pattern of windows and "fins."
(I remember Zoltan Kiss bravely acquiescing
to the bathroom windows being glazed, for
the sake of consistency, in the same manner as
office and seminar windows.)[2] If you walk slowly
around the Quadrangle, see how the spaces
change, opening up and closing down, glancing
across a broad pool or compressing behind a
berm or bosque of trees. Nothing should inter-
rupt the serenity of the Quad.

The third space would allow for some rau-
cous activity. It would be an alternative to the
Mall, serving the sports complex, the student
union and co-op, a cafe and a cinema. With
1,500 students projected, a second lively congre-
gation area was necessary.

The fourth space was introduced into the
program on our initiative. SFU was launched as
a commuter school, but in my experience dormitory life was essential to the rounding out of
one's education and was, in any case, an essential component of all great universities. Thus,
a residential complex to house one-third of
the students was introduced next to the sports
complex. We believed this position appropriate,
for it could link both facilities and encourage
off-hour use. Residences would be complemented
by the unstructured and park like spaces at the
far end of the campus.

My travels in the Far East demonstrated
how even small buildings when cut into a mountain side could become part of the mountain
whereas large ones perched on top were simply
dwarfed by it. By terracing all elements of the

university, its buildings, parking lots, playing fields and landscaping, the earth forms and structures could all become part of one composition—part of the mountain, not stuck on it. The plan also allowed for incremental expansion outward from a spine along the mountain ridge. The spine could connect all present and future buildings, bring services to them, provide parking and access from descending levels. The campus would be infinitely flexible and expandable. It was thoroughly rational and yet, properly respected, would never lose the beauty of being of one piece.

The day of the announcement of the result was bright and sunny.[3] An excited crowd had gathered at Burnaby Mountain Park. Geoff and I had given up hope of winning, for it seemed all we were suggesting was in violation of the rules of the competition. We had resigned ourselves to being right rather than winners and attended the ceremony out of curiosity about our colleagues' work. You can't imagine our utter astonishment when we were not only proclaimed winners but recommended as master planner and designers for the whole campus. The four runners-up would work on separate buildings within our plan and under our design guidance. The summer's activity had been nothing—that September began the most exciting, frustrating and rewarding period of our lives.

We immediately asked Dr. Shrum for four months to reconsider our proposal in a more realistic light, for we knew how rash and romantic it was.[4] He replied, "I'll give you one month and in that time, I will want a plan of how you divide the

university so as to work with the four runners-up.
Not only that, the university is to open two years
from this date."[5] We had no time to reconsider let
alone question our premises for a task we thought
from the beginning impossible. Our joy was
dampened by the enormity of what we had to do.
We didn't know how or where to start. We were
to put into concrete a university for which we had
only an untested, wholly invented plan.

We were soon to become used to Dr.
Shrum's direct and uncompromising approach
and to gain great respect for his clarity of
vision, indomitable will and high principles.
We had the idea and he made it happen. In fact,
he had not been persuaded by our scheme at
first, but once convinced by the jury, was solidly
behind it. Though we were to tremble at many
confrontations with him, he always gave us the
support we needed and respected us for standing up to him. We were lucky, for the university
would never have been built without him.

So the harrowing adventure was launched.
I remember the exhilaration when, after the sur-
veyors had cleared a line through the thick forest,
we climbed stumps to look out and there at the
end of the long swath we could see the green
of Stanley Park and the Lion's Gate Bridge, mag-
ically appearing just as we had predicted. With
great enthusiasm, I wrote a prospectus on the
idea of the university to be circulated for faculty
recruitment.[6] I am afraid I misled many as to what
could be realized in provincial British Columbia.
Carried away by revolutionary zeal, I proposed
a return to the tutorial system modified for vast

numbers of students. Lectures would be few and to large groups, by distinguished professors, but the main teaching vehicle would be seminars of ten to twenty students. I remember the panic as we raced to get our thirty-second scale drawings done to hand over to our four fellow teams.

In the meeting at which we discussed the first phase building program, Dr. Shrum gave us some wise and prescient advice. "Do what is essential now," he said bluntly, "for there will be no opportunity in the future." So Bob Harrison was given the library; Duncan McNab the theatre, gym and swimming pool; Rhone and Iredale the laboratory component; Zoltan Kixss the first half of the Academic Quadrangle. As design coordinators, we chose not a building but the Mall structure that would tie the university together. It included a parking structure, a service trunk to all buildings and a landscaped bridge soaring over the ridges and dips of the mountain top. Certainly, it would never be built in a speculative future. Geoff and I had never done anything much larger than a single house and now we were immersed in the utter confusion of coordinating four architects and five contractors on five contiguous sites. As excavation progressed and foundations were poured it looked as though the whole mountaintop was being reconstructed. We managed by hiring the best people we could find and then bungled through in the fine old tradition.

We were well into the design development phase before President McTaggart-Cowan joined the university and the first faculty members were appointed.[7] The normal process of following the academic programming of the deans and their faculties was forgone altogether.

In the rush, individual requirements were subordinated and the Chancellor and President made all the decisions about space allocations. The deans were left with choosing their furniture and equipment and fitting out their allocated space. But with only one man making all the decisions, things moved with great speed.

With the President came a Board of Governors and gradually decision-making became bureaucratized. Inevitably, no matter how sterling and well-intentioned the Board, matters were no longer as clearly and easily dispatched as before. We had hired a brilliant but unorthodox designer for the Mall roof.[8] While he had a persistent, unequivocable logic and professionalism in his approach, his manner antagonized the contractor of the Mall and undermined his credibility with the President and the Board.[9] As a result, he lost control of decisions that proved vital to the structure much later, in the great snow of 1973.[10]

I remember that everyone who worked on the university felt a sense of euphoria toward the end, exemplified by the Italian tile layers on the Mall. They would race down the Mall with forklifts swaying, singing Neapolitan opera in the mountain air at the top of their lungs. I had to reassure the President that they were not taking the job lightly and would be finished on time.

The university did open as scheduled. We thought that we had all performed the "miracle on Burnaby Mountain." Imperfect and unfinished, SFU could at least begin to function. We were justifiably proud of our "instant university" and completely unprepared for a certain Board meeting at that time. We showed up expecting to be congratulated and instead found ourselves being roundly upbraided for defects in construction, leaks from hasty construction or where the work of two contractors came together, and so on. Afterwards, Geoff and I decided to drown our misery in a good film. Unfortunately, it was [Laurence] Olivier's *Hamlet* and we stumbled out in even deeper despair! For the next few years we seemed to be working under a cloud, but construction continued, the Quad was completed and residences begun.

There was the difficulty in persuading the Chancellor to let us design the landscaping for the Quad, a responsibility I felt essential for realizing the Quad's contemplative purpose. There was the Shell gas station crisis when, to our horror, the best site on the campus, plotted for the student-faculty union, was given over to a gas station. Gratifyingly, the first to recognize this abomination and react were the students who for weeks sported "Shell Out" buttons.[11] There were the inevitable temporary huts—"Shrum's slums" that migrated from UBC and remain to this day. There was the threat of high-rise apartments to which we responded with a low-rise scheme that housed as many as cheaply, and conformed well with the campus. After we showed it to Dr. Shrum, the "developer" disappeared.

There were the days of student unrest and an "occupation" but I was confident that no damage would be done, for the very nature of the university plan defied riot.[12] There was no building that could be targeted as "theirs." Someone later suggested to me that the very urban nature of the campus defused violence, for everyone was crowded into a shared situation and forced to resolve their differences.

Very shortly, the academic record of SFU, though a small and new university, convinced me that the urban quality of the university was indeed stimulating cultural and intellectual activity. The university was a tightly compressed community, a city in miniature. The students that came out had left rural and suburban mildew behind for a more astute attitude towards life.

There came a period when we had little to do with the university at all, and the master plan was contravened. The Education Department went in beyond the Science Block instead of near the gymnasium and consequently the balancing link that would keep the library central to the campus was lost.[13] Everything began to be concentrated at one end instead of distributed more evenly on either side of the library and Mall. For various reasons morale declined, to be reflected in the lack of upkeep, the proliferation of defacing posters, and notices taped everywhere. But that time has passed.

Recently, new leadership has brought new enthusiasm. Everything is looking fresh and well-groomed, as if only just built. I was called back to consult on the master plan and have been involved in the one proposal I have, from the beginning, thought most vital for the

university—a university village.[14] If the number
of commuters could be reduced and a solid body
of residents introduced, the university would
gain a stability and liveliness that would enable it
to offer a complete educational experience. Again,
the model of Al-Azhar returns, where the "real
life" of the streets flowed just under the latticed
windows of the dormitories.With the full university community's endorsement and under
the stewardship of Herb Auerbach, sketch plans
were drawn up as a basis for development of
a 2,160-unit village, to include shops, restaurants,
hotel and conference center, entertainment and
recreation facilities. The village would be open
for rental or lease, not only to students but to
anyone wishing to live near the mountaintop university. University personnel would have priority
but a mixture would be encouraged. At one point
all necessary details were worked out and interested developers were even approached. It needed
one small push from the Federal Government
through the Canadian Mortgage and Housing
Corporation. But it was an unprecedented project that did not fall into a known category and
so was easily tied up in red tape. For the university
to come of age—for British Columbia to come
of age—the village must be built, and in a way
complimentary and supportive to the university.
Only in this way will SFU move again towards
a rendezvous with its destiny.

Long ago now, in the first spring of the
university's life, we were still unjaded and fighting
for perfection. Our landscape plan would have
the fields around the university planted in wild

flowers and grasses, to slope down to a lake at the edge of the forget, giving a bucolic balance and retreat to the campus. But the groundskeeper kept cutting the grass. We became convinced that if we planted wild poppies there, the sight of their colourful blooms would keep the grass cutters away. Here was to be Flower Power in action.

One sunny late April evening, members of our office, several faculty, students and friends gathered about Helen Goodwin, a UBC dance teacher, on the slopes below the theatre. We had twenty pounds of poppy seed and several bottles of Faisca. To each person we gave a yard of red cotton to adorn themselves and a musical instrument, a simple percussion type. In the delicate spring air and splendid colours of the evening, we were overcome by a Bacchic exuberance. In a long procession, with strips of red flying from arms and legs and hair, we snaked and danced and twirled across the fields, around the running track, up the stairs to the Mall and down the Mall to the Quad. But for us, it was deserted. It was a truly pagan rite, and just as the sun was lowering Helen mounted the Quad steps like a high priestess. Each one of us, without bidding, came forward silently to lay our instrument at herfeet as she invoked the setting sun.

At this point, some bewildered tourists wandered onto the Mall. What they saw, like the two spinsters at Versailles,[15] were the ghosts of the original tribe that had built this mountain temple. Their shock was amusing at the time but now it seems that maybe, in reality, they had.

Notes

1   The architectural competition for the SFU campus was held in 1963, with the purpose of choosing one overall winner and four runners-up. Each runner-up would design a section of the university under the supervision of the winner. Erickson and Massey were awarded first place and the runners-up were Rhone and Iredale (William R. Rhone and W. Randle Iredale, second place); Zoltan Kiss (third); Robert F. Harrison (fourth); and Duncan S. McNab and Associates (fifth).

2   Zoltan Kiss (1924–), one of the architects working with Erickson and Massey on the campus design, and responsible for designing and building the Academic Quadrangle.

3   31 July 1963.

4   Gordon Shrum (1896–1985), the first Chancellor of SFU, from 1964 to 1968.

5   The university opened on 9 September 1965.

6   We have been unable to identify this document, however it seems likely that it would echo Erickson's statements about education in this volume, as well as within the 1963 Erickson / Massey Architects planning document for Simon Fraser University.

7   Patrick McTaggart-Cowan (1912–1997), the first president of SFU, from 1964 to 1968.

8   Architect Jeffrey Lindsay (1924–1984), whose involvement with the campus design began in October 1963. Gene Waddell, *The Design for Simon Fraser University and the Problems Accompanying Excellence* (unpublished manuscript, 1998), p. 264. Simon Fraser University Archives, Item no. F-262-1-0-0-0-2.

9   The contractor was John Laing & Son (Canada) Ltd.

10   It seems likely that Erickson has misremembered the date, as the winter of 1968–69 saw the second-highest accumulated snowfall then on record. Referring to the Mall roof, Waddell writes, "in January and February 1969,

unprecedented snowfall caused 45 percent of the glass to break." *The Design for Simon Fraser University and the Problems Accompanying Excellence* (unpublished manuscript, 1998), pp. 304–6: Simon Fraser University Archives, Item no. F-262-1-0-0-0-2. https://atom.archives.sfu.ca/f-262-1-0-0-0-2.

11   These protests occurred in 1966. See Hugh Johnston, *Radical Campus: Making Simon Fraser University* (Toronto: Douglas and McIntyre, 2005), 257–65.

12   Erickson appears to refer to a November 1968 protest over admissions policies regarding transfer credits where students occupied four floors of administration offices. See Johnston, *Radical Campus*, 284.

13   The Education Building was constructed in 1978.

14   Waddell writes: "In 1981 Erickson proposed a third 'master plan for student housing … a mixed housing village carrying out the extended Mall but dissolving into a less formal village complex terracing down the slopes.' Erickson said, 'my whole aim was that it should be as much of a mixed community as possible' including open market housing. 'I think the only thing that is missing which we put into our original scheme … was the village—that it [the University] should be a living community and not a commuting community.' In addition to proposing alternatives for housing, 'there were also two updates of the Master Plan by Alan Bell from my office, one in the 70's and the last in 1990 for a 25,000 student enrollment.' None of these proposals resulted in any construction." *The Design for Simon Fraser University*, 364–5.

15   A reference to the 1901 Moberly–Jourdain Incident, where two visitors to Versailles claimed they had seen eighteenth-century ghosts, Marie-Antoinette among them.

McGill University
Convocation Address

The ceremony of graduation is a "rite of passage"—a coming-of-age celebration after some
years of initiation into the customs, lore and
witchcraft of our culture, under the tutelage
of the various shamans who preside over this
secret society known as the University.

You have now been accepted amongst
the tribal elders into responsible adulthood
to find your own way, having been let into all
the secrets, and given all the knowledge and
powerful magic which our society offers.
At least that is the legend behind this rite
and the reason for this ceremony.

However, there is one way in which our
society differs from all those others in which
rites of passage signal the orderly progression
from one predictable life stage to another,
and that is that all the powerful knowledge
which you have been given to help you on your
way almost on the instance of graduation
will have lost its power and will no longer be
valid. This is because ours is a strangely
restless society ever advancing its boundaries
of knowledge, meaning that whatever can
be learned, by the time it is learned, is already

part of the past. The result is that instead of being a person of knowledge at this moment of umbilical severance with all that information coming out of your ears, you know very little. More precisely, those years spent in accumulating the knowledge of the past have little reference to the present or the future except when you happen to guess well in plotting the trajectory of knowledge from obscure beginnings into unknown destinations. You can only see from where you have come—seldom where you are going, or even where you are at this moment.

But that is not all—it is not only in the dimension of time that your knowledge fails to help you perceive. The University has provided you with fine-honed lenses for viewing the world—and it would seem the finer the lens, the more precise the focus, the more specific the knowledge—yet these lenses are in fact not really instruments of precision at all; they are devices of elimination, and of illusion: first because the ability to focus on one thing implies elimination of all details that may be extraneous or inapplicable; second because such instruments are the lenses of this particular culture, honed not by the fine dust of reality, as we would like to believe, but by the concepts, biases, and prejudices which belong only to this culture. Your lenses are designed to protect your field of vision from the intrusion of any other contrary or non-supportive view of our collective reality.

But there are other views of reality, let me suggest, which you may not support, but may have as much validity from different viewpoints as those of our own culture.

The University, then, is the highly biased perpetrator of our own inescapable traditions of knowledge: the shamans articulate in esoteric terms your own culture in a form of conscious knowledge. The problem is that you emerge from this cultural laundering fully confident that it is a universal expertise that you have to offer, objective, unprejudiced and free from the popular mythology of your culture. Expertise it may be, universal it is not. Though it may seem that you have been openly and fairly exposed to the world—its cultures, politics, science and history— you have been thoroughly versed only in the conceits of your own culture and your own time.

Endless elaboration has bound you to the basic premise of our culture—which is that truth is found exclusively in what can be physi- cally observed or at least decently hypothesized. But often, what is fervently believed as the truth at the time, based on all possible reasonable hypotheses, turns out later to be questionable, disprovable and eventually, in the curve of history, is looked back upon as just another of those irrational myths. Such was the destiny of the flat earth theory and it is possible (and here I make a nervous parry, considering the auspi- cious present company) that we may look back from another future and see modern science, despite all that we know now of its greatness and promise, as only another myth having given us unimaginably greater insights and greater power over our circumstances than any body of knowledge did before but nevertheless following its false promise of reality as alchemy once pursued its fool's gold.

I do not advocate abandoning the directions of our culture, or belittling the importance of our knowledge or our science—by no means. One cannot abandon what has formed the cultural mind and determined its vision—we are inextricably part of our culture. I am only suggesting that just as language, religion, art and politics belong uniquely to a culture, so also does the body of knowledge.

The scientific and materialistic viewpoint of the western world is only one limited cultural way. In the past we fought wars, crusades, dominated whole peoples, wiped out civilizations in the name of our own vision of reality and called it progress. For at least two hundred years it has been our view that has dominated the world, brought mechanization and with it material well-being.

It has been our unchallenged time on earth. But to further persist on our view of progress on this earth against all others is to risk eliminating what little remains of the other great world cultures. Rather we must learn enough about these other premises about reality to accord them our deepest respect. For we have reached a time in history when we badly need some different insights into the human predicament as you graduating today, I'm sure, are well aware.

From our scientific and industrialized point of view it may seem to us that agricultural societies such as those of Southeast Asia, or Africa, are less advanced, more backward and underprivileged than our own. But it has been my experience, in many years of trying to open myself to other cultures, that this is not so—that on the contrary they are advanced where we are backward and are underprivileged only when measured by our yardstick of material well-being.

We have come to realize that what we once thought barbaric, superstitious, pagan, primitive and thus tried to "enlighten" was maybe not so, and perhaps should not have been converted or assimilated. Still we hear the voices of the emerging nations, and of our own native peoples, demanding to be heard. They speak with some resentment, for they are rediscovering the value of their own cultures which they had been persuaded to abandon for westernization. They speak with increasing doubt and misgiving about what we had always held fervently to be the ultimate reality, the only true way. For, although our way may have taken the world further towards human deification than any other in the past, it is also taking us nearer universal calamity measured in terms of pollution, resource depletion, and even extinction of the very sources of life.

It always remained a mystery and a source of consternation to western missionaries how in both China and Japan it was possible to hold simultaneously many beliefs, so that in Asia a Christian convert could still remain a Buddhist, a Taoist and maybe a Shaman at the same time without internal or external distress or discomfort, except to his missionary teacher. I might even suggest that the Islamic-Christian-Judaic idea of one God was maybe a step not forward as we would like to believe, but backward from the comprehensive deification of nature to the isolation and deification of the individual man.

Oriental eclecticism is a form of wisdom which we all must respect—for it teaches us that each way sheds a little light on the truth from a slightly different angle—that there are many roads leading to the same place, and each must be travelled in order to know that place in its totality.

Fifteen years ago, having been thoroughly schooled in the western traditions of art and architecture here at McGill, in Europe, and around the Mediterranean, I stood in a temple garden in Japan completely mystified and bewildered. Nothing in my background had prepared me for the fragile pavilions that seemed too precious, the miniature worlds of nature that seemed too artful in that temple garden. But standing there, dreamily watching the squads of gardeners rustling through the foliage, I was suddenly struck by the fact that with all their work they had changed nothing—only that after they had gone every tree seemed to have been unburdened, to breathe more freely, to reach out more gracefully—yet without change— merely a realization of its full potential. It was a moment of insight for me. I suddenly saw the other side of that coin of which until then I had known only one face. The face that I knew measured any act of art or architecture, music or manners, in human terms by means of the aesthetic of the human body—while the face on the other side of the coin measured all art in nature' s terms—the aesthetic of grass and trees. Each from its premise established a whole scale of values quite the opposite of the other, each perpetrating a great art having little or no relationship to the other. From that day on I learned to seek out, to understand and respect other points of view.

We have a difficult task because we must not only cease to impose our view on other cultures, we must also learn from them a larger and deeper view of reality than our own can give. The hard truth is that we can no longer afford to view the world from the narrow standpoint of westernindustrialized culture, for ours is a culture of fragmentation—theirs a culture of totalities.

In our relentless curiosity about the physical world, our western culture began to develop some 500 years ago the scientific method and with it its corollary—mechanization. By observation, dissection and analysis, we broke down physical phenomena into their function-ing parts, theorized how they worked, and then imitated these processes in our machines. It was a brilliant achievement, but in the pro-cess, fragmentation and analysis became a habit of thought so endemic in our culture that we lost the capability to conceptualize in totalities. It is in the light of this incapacity, therefore, that other cultures based on comprehensive views of reality have more and more meaning for us.

Hopefully, we may begin to see through the eyes of the African, the Indian, the Southeast Asian, the Chinese, learning not tolerance or sympathy, which is condescending, but deep respect for their comprehensive consciousness which can guide us to a deeper understanding of our own culture and perhaps show us the way to put the fragments back together. We must gain the vision of wholeness in variety. For human culture is and must remain diverse and various, with many of its facets diametrically opposite to others but complementing one another as black and white, blue and orange, green and red complement one another on the spectrum of colours. It is not our mission to go about the world showing other societies how to do things: rather to learn how to do things better ourselves—and not only do but be—learn to be healed into wholeness.

To learn one must first unlearn, and this is the difficulty—to begin by challenging the basic precepts of our civilization so that we can accept other attitudes without losing our own. The old icons of individualism, of progress, of science may have to be set aside in order that other forms may become open to our view. The reward to be gained from a true respect for other cultures is not only preparation for a necessary new human culture, but is also insight into our own culture—a perspective on it, and a respect for its integrity.

Therefore, in this last of your lectures, I challenge you—graduates of the old order—to enter into the new!

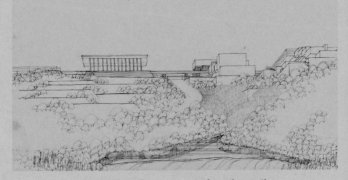

Approach to the centre gate from the south

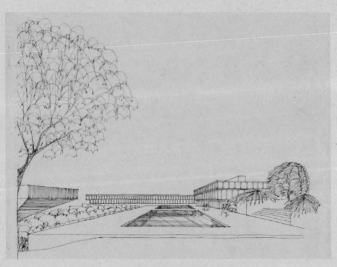

The east gate

Perspective towards the Academic Quadrangle
and cafeteria from the Mall

Erickson / Massey Architects, fragment of a competition
drawing presenting perspectives and sections of the
Simon Fraser University project, ca. 1964.
Arthur Erickson fonds, CCA Collection, ARCH258568.
Gift of the Erickson Family.

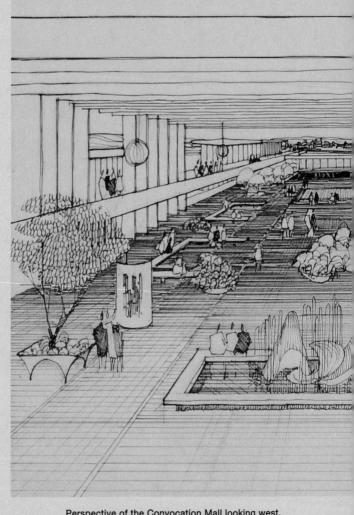

Perspective of the Convocation Mall looking west,
with library entrance on the right

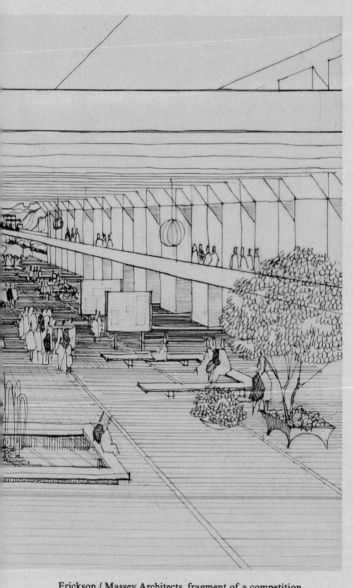

Erickson / Massey Architects, fragment of a competition
drawing presenting perspectives and sections of the
Simon Fraser University project, ca. 1964.
Arthur Erickson fonds, CCA Collection, ARCH258568.
Gift of the Erickson Family.

View of Convocation Mall and library entrance in the background

Simon Fraser University, Presentation booklet (October 1966), page 8.
Arthur Erickson fonds, CCA Collection, ARCH279734.
Photograph by Peter Knowlden / SFU Audio-Visual Centre

View of the Mall looking east,
with the Academic Quadrangle in the background

Simon Fraser University, Presentation booklet (October 1966), page 19.
Arthur Erickson fonds, CCA Collection, ARCH279734.
Photograph by Peter Knowlden / SFU Audio-Visual Centre

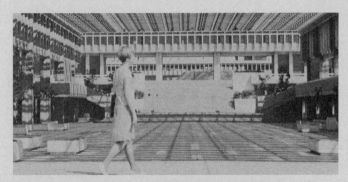

View of Convocation Mall looking east
with Academic Quadrangle in the background

An open-air lecture at the Central Mall

A quiet place to read in the Central Mall

Simon Fraser University, Presentation booklet
(October 1966), pages 9–13.

View of the Mall

Exhibition viewing

A quiet place to read in the Central Mall

Arthur Erickson on Learning Systems
With an introduction by Melanie O'Brian

Canadian Centre for Architecture
Concordia University Press

Editorial Group   Meredith Carruthers, Albert Ferré,
                   Natasha Leeman, Geoffrey Robert Little,
                   Ryan Van Huijstee

Graphic Design   Sean Yendrys

Research   Natalie Greenberg, Thomas Molander,
                  Swapnaa Tamhane

Concordia University Press gratefully acknowledges the
generous support of the Birks Family Foundation,
the Estate of Linda Kay, and the Estate of Tanneke De Zwart.

The Canadian Centre for Architecture thanks the Estate of
Arthur Erickson for its collaboration and continued support.

Printed and bound in Germany by PögeDruck, Leipzig
and Buchbinderei Mönch.

This book is printed on Forest Stewardship Council certified
paper and meets the permanence of paper requirements
of ANSI/NISO Z39.48-1992.

Concordia University Press's books are available
for free on several digital platforms.
Visit www.concordia.ca/press

First English edition published in 2022
10 9 8 7 6 5 4 3 2 1

978-1-988111-31-5 Paper
978-1-988111-32-2 E-book

Library and Archives Canada Cataloguing in Publication
Title: Arthur Erickson on learning systems.
Other titles: On learning systems
Names: Erickson, Arthur, 1924-2009, author. | Centre
canadien d'architecture, publisher.
Description: Series statement: Building arguments |
Includes bibliographical references.
Identifiers: Canadiana 20210240946 | ISBN 9781988111315
(softcover)
Subjects: LCSH: Erickson, Arthur, 1924-2009. | LCSH:
Architecture—Study and teaching (Higher)—
    British Columbia—Burnaby. | LCSH: Instructional sys-
tems—British Columbia—Burnaby. | LCSH: Simon
    Fraser University—History. | LCSH: Simon Fraser
University—Buildings.
Classification: LCC NA2305.C3 S56 2022 | DDC
720.071/171133—dc23

Canadian Centre for Architecture
1920 rue Baile
Montréal, Québec H3H 2S6

Concordia University Press
1455 de Maisonneuve Blvd. W.
Montreal, Quebec H3G 1M8

Arthur Erickson (1924–2009) was one of Canada's most important and influential architects. Significant projects include Simon Fraser University in Burnaby, BC; Vancouver's Robson Square; the Canadian Chancery in Washington, DC; Napp Laboratories in Cambridge, UK; and Toronto's Roy Thomson Hall.

Melanie O'Brian is a curator of contemporary art.